Wise Words from

Female Sporting Heroes

Harper *by* Design

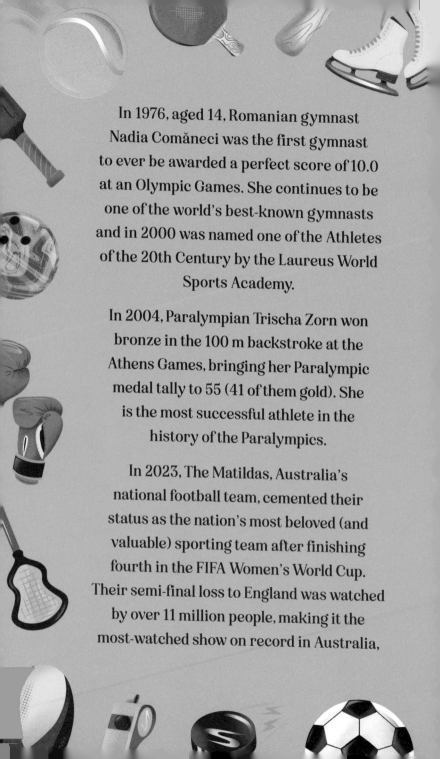

In 1976, aged 14, Romanian gymnast Nadia Comăneci was the first gymnast to ever be awarded a perfect score of 10.0 at an Olympic Games. She continues to be one of the world's best-known gymnasts and in 2000 was named one of the Athletes of the 20th Century by the Laureus World Sports Academy.

In 2004, Paralympian Trischa Zorn won bronze in the 100 m backstroke at the Athens Games, bringing her Paralympic medal tally to 55 (41 of them gold). She is the most successful athlete in the history of the Paralympics.

In 2023, The Matildas, Australia's national football team, cemented their status as the nation's most beloved (and valuable) sporting team after finishing fourth in the FIFA Women's World Cup. Their semi-final loss to England was watched by over 11 million people, making it the most-watched show on record in Australia, and no doubt contributing to the Australian National Dictionary Centre's announcement of 'Matilda' as the 2023 Word of the Year.

Globally it might seem like women's sport is currently having a moment – a record crowd of 92,000 people attended a US women's college volleyball game in September 2023 – but throughout history it's clear that female athletes have always been leading the way: breaking through glass ceilings, demanding equality and inspiring all of us to do, and be, better.

As former Australian footballer and broadcaster Craig Foster said, 'Sport creates, contributes to and shapes culture and national identity'. That spirit is reflected in this collection of quotes from a variety of global sportswomen who have helped shift the conversation forward in a myriad of ways. We salute them for their incredible sporting achievements and for the great work they do beyond sport.

Victory is very, very sweet. It tastes better than any dessert you've ever had.

Serena Williams

Tennis player

Winner of 23 Grand Slam women's singles titles;
highest-earning female athlete of all time

I think athletes are perfectionists, especially swimmers. It comes down to milliseconds, your turns, your skills ... you want to get it perfect.

Emma McKeon

Swimmer

Australia's most decorated Olympian,
with 11 medals, including five gold;
eight-time world-record holder

Dreams weigh nothing.

Sam Kerr

Footballer

Australia's leading goal scorer (male or female);
only female footballer to have won the Golden
Boot in leagues on three different continents

The ocean humbles you. You can go and win a world title, but you're never going to beat the ocean.

Stephanie Gilmore

Surfer

Eight-time world champion on the
Women's WSL World Tour

11

You will not always be strong, but you can always be brave.

Simone Biles

Gymnast

Most decorated gymnast in history,
with 23 World Championship and four
Olympic gold medals

12

Instead of focusing on what I didn't like about my body or my limitations, I chose to be grateful for the remarkable body that I have.

Bethany Hamilton

Surfer

Returned to competitive surfing less than three months after losing her left arm in a shark attack in 2003

Champions adjust. Champions are masters at being resilient.

Billie Jean King

Tennis player

Winner of 39 Grand Slam titles; famously
won the 'Battle of the Sexes' tennis match
against Bobby Riggs

How small we' are compared to nature.

Edurne Pasaban

Mountain climber

Became the first woman to climb the 14 highest peaks in the world in 2010

19

Celebrate what you've accomplished, but also raise the bar a little higher each time you succeed.

Mia Hamm

Footballer

Two-time Olympic gold medallist and two-time
FIFA Women's World Cup champion; first woman
inducted into the World Football Hall of Fame

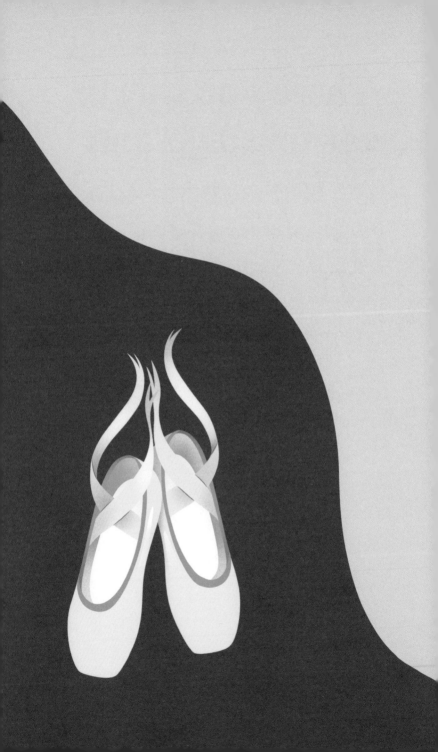

There's no way to go on stage and be the dancer and the artist you want to be if you're not prepared, focused and grounded.

Misty Copeland

Ballerina

First African-American woman to be
promoted to principal dancer for the
American Ballet Theatre, in 2015

The' triumph can't be had without the struggle.

Wilma Rudolph

Sprinter

Overcame childhood polio to become the first
American woman to win three gold medals
in a single Olympics, at Rome 1960

24

Dreams and visions give us strength, setbacks are inevitable. It takes a strong will to win.

Jutta Kleinschmidt

Rally driver

First woman to win the Dakar Rally, in 2001

27

Everyone is equal, on and off the field. For girls in particular, [rugby] boosts their confidence and inspires leadership.

Charlotte Caslick

Rugby union player

Won gold at the 2022 Commonwealth Games,
2022 Rugby Sevens World Cup and 2016 Rio Olympics

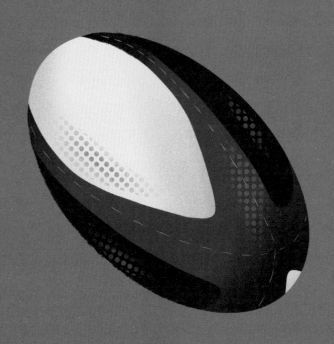

'Not all of us can
be pro athletes and
play for our country
... [but] every single
one of us can figure
out what makes
us feel good about
ourselves.

Abby Wambach

Footballer

Two-time Olympic gold medallist and a
FIFA Women's World Cup champion; scored
184 goals at international level, the second
highest of all players (male or female)

If you can't dream big, ridiculous dreams, what's the point in dreaming at all?

Ronda Rousey

Mixed martial artist and wrestler

First American woman to win an Olympic medal
in judo, in Beijing 2008; only woman to be the
champion in both the UFC and WWE

'You don't fear for your life in the middle of a storm; you can't really afford to.

Ellen MacArthur

Sailor

Broke the record for fastest person to sail
around the world, in 2005

Technique and ability alone do not get you to the top; it is the willpower that is most important.

Junko Tabei

Mountain climber

First woman to summit Mount Everest,
in 1975, and first woman to climb the highest
peak on every continent

To me, the sea is like a person ... when I swim in the sea, I talk to it. I never feel alone when I'm out there.

Gertrude Ederle

Long-distance swimmer

First woman to swim across the
English Channel, in 1926

No one can arrive from being talented alone. God gives talent; work transforms talent into genius.

Ballerina

First ballerina to tour the world; the solo dance
The Dying Swan was created for her

When the pursuit of natural harmony is a shared journey, great heights can be attained.

Lynn Hill

Rock climber

First person in the world (male or female) to
free-climb The Nose – a steep, exposed route
on Yosemite's legendary El Capitan

I'm strong, I'm tough, [but] I still wear my eyeliner.

Lisa Leslie

Basketballer

Four-time Olympic gold medallist and two-time
WNBA champion; first player to slam-dunk in
a WNBA game, in 2002

No one should have to justify the space that they take up, and people with disability shouldn't have to be exceptional in order to be accepted.

Madison de Rozario

Wheelchair racer

Two-time Paralympic gold medallist;
current world-record holder in the women's
800 m T53 category

Cry in the beginning so you can smile in the end.

Marta Vieira da Silva

Footballer

Only footballer to have won the FIFA World Player
of the Year five times consecutively

48

I've always wanted to win at anything that I do.

Meg Lanning

Cricketer

Seven-time World Cup champion; holds
the record for the most Women's One Day
International centuries

51

Age is no barrier. It's a limitation you put on your mind.

Jackie Joyner-Kersee

Heptathlete and long jumper

Won three gold, one silver and two bronze
medals over four Olympic Games

52

My ancestors were the first people to walk on this land. Those' other girls were always going to come up against my ancestors. Who's going to stop me?

Cathy Freeman

Sprinter

Won an Olympic gold medal in the 400 m, in Sydney 2000; two-time World Championship gold medallist

I've got a 'fearless' tattoo on my foot so I can see that before I dive.

Ariarne Titmus

Swimmer

Two-time Olympic and six-time
World Championship gold medallist

Women can do anything and we can beat the world.

Michelle Payne

Jockey

First and only female jockey to win
a Melbourne Cup, in 2015

'When I'm on the court, I feel like I'm in my element.

Lauren Jackson

Basketballer

Represented Australia at four Olympic Games,
winning three silver medals and one bronze;
five-time WNBA champion

I don't run away from a challenge [when] I am afraid. Instead, I run toward it, because the only way to escape fear is to trample it beneath your feet.

Nadia Comăneci

Gymnast

Five-time Olympic gold medallist; first gymnast to score a perfect 10.0 in an Olympic event, aged 14

If you are going to own your success ... Then you have to be willing to own your failures.

Swimmer

Four-time Olympic and four-time
World Championship gold medallist

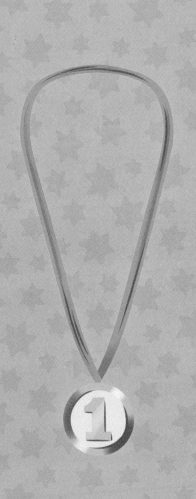

If I can be relaxed and have fun, then I can get the most out of myself.

Torah Bright

Snowboarder

Australia's most successful Winter Olympian,
winning one gold medal, in Vancouver 2010,
and one silver medal, in Sochi 2014; two-time
Winter X Games gold medallist

When you play your best is when you are bringing out the best in each other.

Liz Watson

Netballer

Won gold medals at the 2022 Commonwealth
Games and 2023 Netball World Cup

I want to look back and know that I contributed positively to successful teams and left nothing out there on the park.

Alyssa Healy

Cricketer

Has represented Australia since 2010; two-time
ICC Women's T20I Cricketer of the Year

'Be the best footballer you can be, be the best person you can be.

Mary Fowler

Footballer

Represented Australia from age 15, played at
two FIFA Women's World Cups

72

If you truly want to live life you have to get involved, pursue your passions and dream big.

Sailor

Became the youngest person to sail around
the world non-stop, solo and unassisted
in 2010, aged 16

'When anyone tells me I can't do anything ... I'm just not listening any more.

Florence Griffith Joyner

Sprinter

Fastest woman ever recorded – her 100 m and
200 m world records have stood since 1988

76

I've always believed that I could do whatever I set my mind to do.
I encourage women to work harder and fight harder.

Alice Coachman

High jumper

First Black woman to win an Olympic gold medal, at London 1948

Don't be coy and just shoot.

Archer

First archer (male or female) to win three gold
medals at a single Olympics, at Tokyo 2020

The sky is my limit, because I never know how high I can jump.

Yelena Isinbayeva

Pole vaulter

Two-time Olympic and eight-time World
Championship gold medallist; first woman
to clear 5 metres

83

The moment of victory is too short to live for that alone.

Martina Navratilova

Tennis player

Winner of 59 major titles,
the most in the Open Era

84

'It's all about who can have the most fun. I try to have fun and pull off the tricks I want to do. That's how I go about it.

Momiji Nishiya

Skateboarder

Won an Olympic gold medal aged just 13,
at Tokyo 2020

Each one of us has a fire in our heart for something. It's our goal in life to find it and keep it lit.

Mary Lou Retton

Gymnast

Won five Olympic medals, including one gold,
at Los Angeles 1984

My stubborn streak pushed me to overcome obstacles that were placed in front of me.

Trischa Zorn

Swimmer

Most decorated Paralympian in history, winning 41 gold medals, nine silver and five bronze over seven Paralympic Games

I want to do with skates what Fred Astaire is doing with dancing.

Sonja Henie

Figure skater

Three-time Olympic and ten-time World
Championship gold medallist; winner of
more Olympic and World titles than any
other female figure skater

At the beginning, it's all you have: a simple forehand, a simple backhand. It's all you have at the end, too.

Maria Sharapova

Tennis player

One of only ten women to achieve the Career Grand Slam: winning all four major championships during the course of a career

Harper *by* Design
An imprint of HarperCollins*Publishers*

HarperCollins*Publishers*
Australia • Brazil • Canada • France • Germany • Holland • India
Italy • Japan • Mexico • New Zealand • Poland • Spain • Sweden
Switzerland • United Kingdom • United States of America

HarperCollins acknowledges the Traditional Custodians of the lands upon which
we live and work, and pays respect to Elders past and present.

First published on Gadigal Country in Australia in 2024
by HarperCollins*Publishers* Australia Pty Limited
ABN 36 009 913 517
harpercollins.com.au

Compilation copyright © HarperCollins*Publishers* Australia Pty Limited 2024

A catalogue record for this book is available from the National Library of Australia.

ISBN 978 1 4607 6614 9 (hardback)

Publisher: Mark Campbell
Publishing Director: Brigitta Doyle
Editors: Jess Cox and Rachel Dennis
Designer: Mietta Yans, HarperCollins Design Studio
Illustrator: Lynn Bremner
Colour reproduction by Splitting Image Colour Studio, Clayton VIC
Printed and bound in China by RR Donnelley

8 7 6 5 4 3 2 1   24 25 26 27